For Brooks Brigmon—D.D.M.

For a great kid named Adam Robert—J.D.

Text © 2006 Dandi Daley Mackall. Illustrations © 2006 Jane Dippold.

© 2006 Standard Publishing, Cincinnati, Ohio.

A division of Standex International Corporation.

All rights reserved. No part of this book may be reproduced

in any form, except for brief quotations in reviews,

without the written permission of the publisher. Printed in China.

Project editor: Robin Stanley.

Cover and interior design: Marissa Bowers.

All Scripture quotations, unless otherwise indicated,

are taken from the Holy Bible, New Living Translation, copyright © 1996.

Used by permission of Tyndale House Publishers, Inc., Wheaton, IL. 60189.

All rights reserved.

13 12 11 10 09 08 07 06   9 8 7 6 5 4 3 2 1

Library of Congress Cataloging-in-Publication Data

Mackall, Dandi Daley.

The golden rule / written by Dandi Daley Mackall ; pictures by Jane Dippold.

p. cm. -- (My favorite verses)

ISBN 0-7847-1822-9 (casebound picture book)

1. Golden rule--Juvenile literature. 2. Bible. N.T. Matthew VII, 12--Juvenile literature.

I. Dippold, Jane. II. Title. III. Series: Mackall, Dandi Daley. My favorite verses.

BV4715.M33 2006   226.2'0520836--dc22   2006000023

I'll walk with Jesus and follow
THE GOLDEN RULE

Written by Dandi Daley Mackall   Pictures by Jane Dippold

Standard® PUBLISHING
Bringing The Word to Life
Cincinnati, Ohio

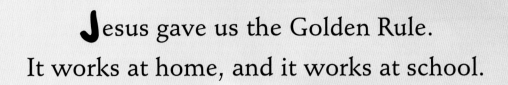

Jesus gave us the Golden Rule.
It works at home, and it works at school.

Treat your friends and
the whole world, too,
the way you wish that
they treated you.

Do for others what you would like them to do for you.

Matthew 7:12

If I win a game that my buddies lose,
I will put myself in my buddies' shoes,
'cause when I don't win, I can get the blues.

I'll follow the Golden Rule.

Do for others what you would like them to do for you.

Matthew 7:12

In a thunderstorm on a cold, dark night,
if my sister cries, I can hold her tight—
'cause when I get scared, holding feels just right.

I'll follow the Golden Rule.

Do for others what you would like them to do for you.

Matthew 7:12

When a new kid's shy on a Saturday,
I'll remember times when I felt that way.

And I'll ask that girl if she'd like to play.

I'll follow the Golden Rule.

At my granny's house, Granny's on her own.
So I call her up on the telephone.
'Cause I don't think I'd like to be alone,

I'll follow the Golden Rule.

Do for others what you would like them to do for you.
Matthew 7:12

When my mom and I take the bus downtown,
I'll return a smile when I get a frown—
for a smile feels good when you're feeling down.

I'll follow the Golden Rule.

Do for others what you would like them to do for you.

Matthew 7:12

I can help my brother—
he's a little tyke—

when he's kind of shaky
on his two-wheeled bike . . .

'Cause if I were wobbly,
help is what I'd like!

I'll follow the Golden Rule.

Do for others what you would like them to do for you.

Matthew 7:12

Well, it never hurts to be on my guard
when my dad mows grass, or he weeds our yard.
'Cause I like his help when MY chores are hard,

I'll follow the Golden Rule.

Do for others what you would like them to do for you.

Matthew 7:12

If a bigger kid tries to pick on me,
or we're head to head,
but we can't agree,

I'll be just as kind as I wish he'd be—

and follow the Golden Rule.

Do for others what you would like them to do for you.

Matthew 7:12

In the grocery store, everyone I see
is a smiling, waving opportunity.
Do you see that girl waving back at me

when I follow
the Golden Rule?

Do for others what you would like them to do for you.

Matthew 7:12

That's the Golden Rule, and it's here to stay!
Jesus made the rule, and he showed the way.
So I'll walk with him every single day—

and follow the Golden Rule.

Matthew 7:12

Do for others

what you would like them to do for you.